D1379044

Badge
F·U·N

PETRA BOASE

LORENZ BOOKS
NEW YORK · LONDON · SYDNEY · BATH

First published in 1996 by Lorenz Books

Lorenz Books is an imprint of Anness Publishing Inc.
27 West 20th Street
New York, New York 10011

ISBN 1 85967 318 X

Publisher: Joanna Lorenz
Senior Children's Books Editor: Sue Grabham
Assistant Editor: Sophie Warne
Photographer: John Freeman
Designer: Michael R. Carter

Printed in China

10 9 8 7 6 5 4 3 2 1

Introduction

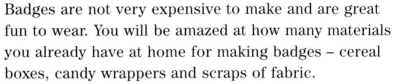

Badges are not very expensive to make and are great fun to wear. You will be amazed at how many materials you already have at home for making badges – cereal boxes, candy wrappers and scraps of fabric.

As well as wearing the badges on your clothes, you could jazz up a hat or a bag with them. Always make sure the badge pin is secure before trying it on, or your badge might fall off. Badges also make great presents for your friends and family.

Before you get to work making badges, it is very important to prepare your work area. Cover the surface you are working on with newspaper to avoid making a mess, and make sure you have all the materials you will need at hand. If you need any help or advice, ask an adult.

Follow the instructions carefully and have lots of fun making your masterpieces!

Petra Boase

Contents

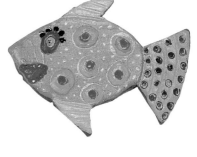

Materials

BUTTONS
These come in all shapes, sizes and colors. Look in secondhand stores for old buttons or simply buy them from a sewing store.

COTTON
This can be purchased at drug stores. It can be glued onto cardboard.

CRÊPE PAPER
This comes in a range of bright colors. It is strong, slightly stretchy and good for making paper flowers.

FABRIC PAINT
This is great for decorating fabric, but remember to let it dry thoroughly before touching it.

FELT
This is a very easy fabric to use, as it doesn't fray and is easy to cut. When gluing it onto cardboard, use only a small amount of glue.

FIMO
This comes in a range of colors. It is important to read the instructions before using it.

FOIL WRAPPERS
These can be saved from candies and chocolate bars. Gently smooth them out and cover your badge shape with them.

GEMSTONES
These are used for decoration and can be purchased from craft and art stores.

GLITTER
This can be glued onto projects as decoration. If there is any left over, it can be poured back into the tube.

GRASS PAPER
This is paper that looks like grass. You can buy it at craft stores. If you can't find any, green felt makes a good alternative.

NEWSPAPER
Save old newspapers and tear them into small squares for making papier-mâché. Lay sheets of newspaper onto the surface you are working on to protect it.

PAINTS
There are all sorts of different paints, so it is important to read the instructions on the tubes or bottles to make sure they are suitable for the project you are painting.

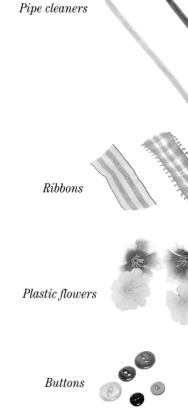

Pipe cleaners

Ribbons

Plastic flowers

Buttons

PIPE CLEANERS
These come in an assortment of colors and can be coiled and bent to make fun shapes. They will need to be attached with a strong glue.

PLASTIC FLOWERS
These can be cut off at the stem and glued onto the badge.

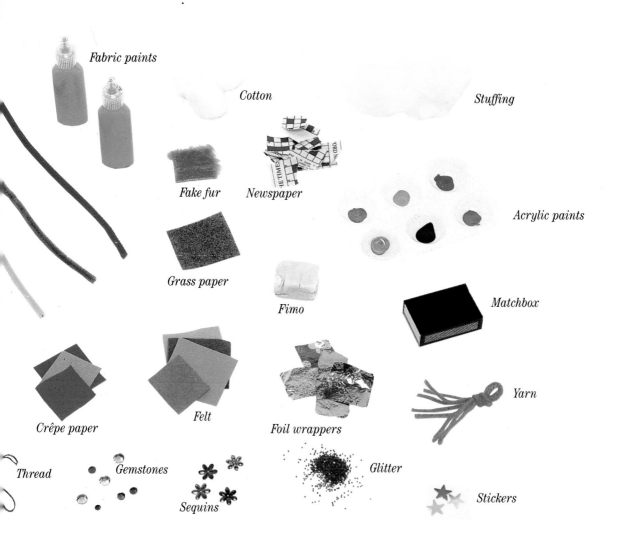

Fabric paints

Cotton

Stuffing

Fake fur

Newspaper

Acrylic paints

Grass paper

Fimo

Matchbox

Crêpe paper

Felt

Foil wrappers

Yarn

Thread

Gemstones

Sequins

Glitter

Stickers

RIBBONS
These come in all sorts of colors and widths. They can be used for making bows to decorate your badges.

SEQUINS
These are shiny and can be glued or sewn onto the surface of your badges.

STICKERS
These come in all sorts of fun colors, shapes, sizes and images. They are great for decoration.

STUFFING
You can buy special types of stuffing for filling fabric shapes. If you don't have any, scrunched-up paper is a good substitute.

Equipment

BADGE PINS
These come in a range of sizes and can be bought at most craft stores. If you are unable to find any, use safety pins instead.

CARDBOARD
You can save thin cardboard from empty cereal boxes.

COLORED PAPER
This comes in a range of wonderful colors. Always keep the small scraps, as you never know when they might be useful.

COMPASS
This is used to make small holes and draw perfect circles. If you don't have one, draw around a cup or plate.

COOKIE CUTTERS
These come in a range of fun shapes. Use them to cut shapes out of dough. If you have borrowed them from the kitchen, remember to clean them thoroughly before returning them.

ELECTRICAL TAPE
This strong tape is very useful for securing pins onto the backs of your badges and is great for decoration.

MASKING TAPE
This isn't as strong as electrical tape, but it is useful for holding things together temporarily.

MODELING TOOLS
These are used for cutting and shaping clay, salt dough or fimo.

NEEDLE
This is used to sew with. The point is very sharp, so be careful.

PAINTBRUSH
Paintbrushes come in a range of sizes and thicknesses. Remember to wash them thoroughly after you have finished using them.

PAPER FASTENERS
These can be pierced through paper or cardboard to hold them together.

PENCIL
You will need a lead pencil for tracing the templates in this book.

PINS
These are used for holding pieces of fabric together while sewing. The points are sharp, so be careful. If you are unsure, always ask an adult to help you.

Colored tape

Scissors

ROLLING PIN
This is useful for rolling out the modeling material.

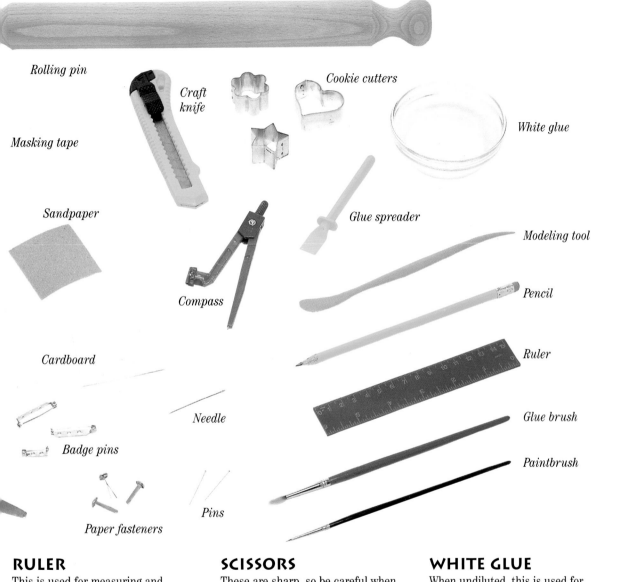

Rolling pin

Craft knife

Cookie cutters

White glue

Masking tape

Sandpaper

Glue spreader

Modeling tool

Compass

Pencil

Cardboard

Ruler

Needle

Glue brush

Badge pins

Paintbrush

Paper fasteners

Pins

RULER

This is used for measuring and drawing straight lines.

SCISSORS

These are sharp, so be careful when cutting paper or fabric. Always sit down when using scissors, and point them away from your body.

WHITE GLUE

When undiluted, this is used for sticking all sorts of different materials together. It can be diluted with water to make papier-mâché.

How to Make Salt Dough

YOU WILL NEED

11 ounces flour
11 ounces salt
7 ounces water
2 tablespoons vegetable oil

1 Measure the ingredients. Put the flour and salt into a bowl and mix well.

2 Gradually pour the water over the salt and flour. Mix well.

4 Take the salt dough out of the bowl and place it on a clean surface that has been dusted with flour. Knead the dough until it is firm and put it in an air-tight container or wrap it in plastic wrap. Put it in the fridge for half an hour before using it.

3 Now pour the vegetable oil over the mixture and mix it in well.

How to Make Papier-Mâché

YOU WILL NEED

Newspaper
White glue
Water

1️⃣ Tear up sheets of newspaper into small pieces

2️⃣ Add water to the white glue, a bit at a time, until you have a runny paste. Stick newspaper into the paste and then onto the cardboard. You will need to apply approximately three to four layers of newspaper. Let the papier-mâché dry overnight in a dry, warm place.

3️⃣ Paint the papier-mâché shape. When the paint has dried, add a layer of varnish for extra protection. You can use either a water-based varnish, or a mixture of white glue and water.

Tracing Templates

1 Place a piece of tracing paper over the template and draw around the shape using a pencil.

2 Take the tracing paper off the template and turn it over. Rub over the traced image with a pencil on the reverse side of the paper.

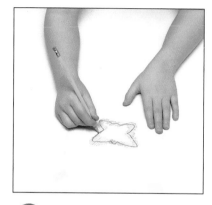

3 Place the tracing paper onto a piece of cardboard or paper with the rubbed side facing down. Draw over the shape you traced with a pencil to transfer the picture.

4 Remove the tracing paper and cut out the shape. Draw around the cardboard shape on the material you are using to make the badge.

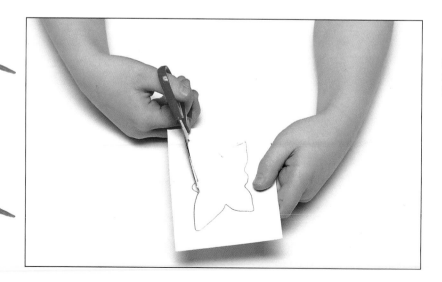

Feathery Chicken

Felt Scotty Dog

Papier-Mâché Cat

Watch this cat's eyes twinkle under bright lights. The gemstones used for the eyes can be purchased at most craft and art stores.

1 Draw a cat's head on cardboard and cut it out. Cover it with three layers of papier-mâché. Leave it in a warm place overnight so that the papier-mâché dries and hardens.

2 Paint both sides of the cat and allow to dry. Varnish the front with a water-based varnish or a mixture of white glue and water.

3 Cut out two small felt triangles and glue them onto the cat's ears. Glue on gemstones for eyes. Cut three pieces of pipe cleaner, approximately 1½ inches long, and glue on to make whiskers. Glue a button onto the center of the pipe cleaners and hold in place for a few minutes until the glue dries.

4 Paint eyelashes around the eyes and paint a line around the felt ears with black paint.

5 Glue the badge pin onto the back of the cat, toward the top of the head. Let dry, and secure the pin with electrical tape before trying on the badge.

Speedy Car

This badge will impress your friends, since the wheels actually move. Why not paint your friends or family on the windows of the car, or cut up old photographs and stick them on?

YOU WILL NEED
Pencil
Cardboard
Ruler
Compass
Scissors
Acrylic paints
Paintbrush
Paper fasteners
White glue and glue brush
Badge pin
Electrical tape

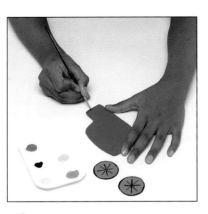

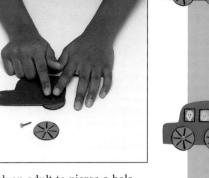

1 Draw a car shape on cardboard. It should be about 4½ inches long by 3 inches high. Use a compass to draw two wheels, about 1½ inches in diameter. Cut out the shapes and paint them. Let dry.

2 Cut out three pieces of cardboard 1 inch by 1 inch and paint a picture of a friend or member of your family on each square. Let the paint dry.

3 Ask an adult to pierce a hole through the center of each wheel with the point of a compass. Push a paper fastener through each wheel and make holes in the car for the paper fasteners to go through. Attach the wheels quite loosely, so they will spin around.

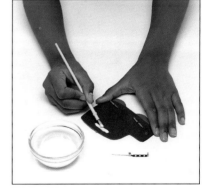

4 Glue the badge pin onto the back of the car and let it dry. Secure the pin with electrical tape before trying on your badge.

Feathery Chicken

This lovable chicken has felt feathers. If you have lots of scraps of different-colored felt you could make a multicolored chicken.

YOU WILL NEED

Pencil
Tracing paper
Cardboard
Scissors
Acrylic paints
Paintbrush
Felt
Felt-tip pen
White glue and glue brush
Pipe cleaners
Ruler
Badge pin
Electrical tape

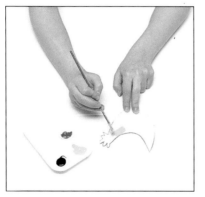

1. Trace the template for the chicken. Transfer the shape onto a piece of cardboard and cut it out. Paint the cardboard yellow.

2. When the paint has dried, paint on the chicken's face.

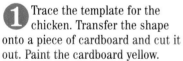

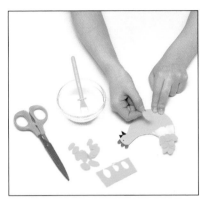

3 Trace the template for the feathers. Transfer the oval onto a scrap of cardboard and cut it out. Draw around the shape on yellow felt using a felt-tip pen. Starting at the tail, glue the felt feathers on the chicken so they overlap each other.

4 Cut two lengths of pipe cleaner approximately 1 inch long for the legs of the chicken. Glue them onto the back of the chicken.

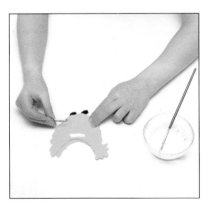

5 Draw around the chicken on a piece of yellow felt using a felt-tip pen. Cut the shape out and glue it onto the back of the chicken. Glue the badge pin onto the back of the badge towards the top of the chicken. Let dry and secure with electrical tape.

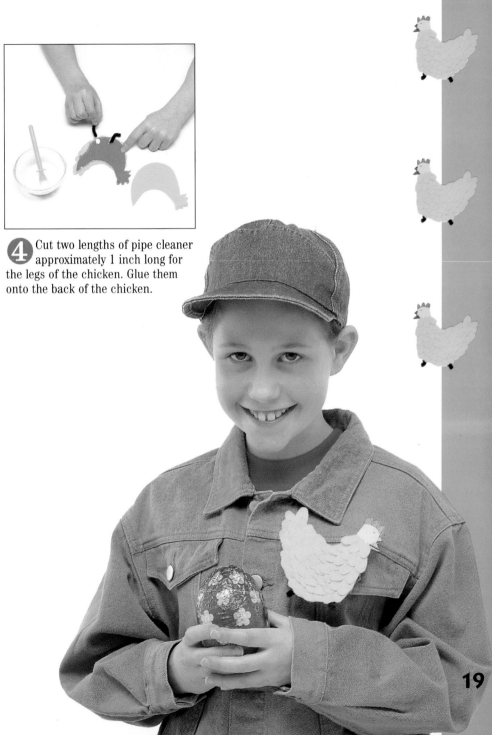

19

Magic Chest

Store your small treasures in this magic chest and keep them close to you at all times!

YOU WILL NEED

Matchbox
Craft knife
Ruler
Masking tape
Shiny paper
White glue and glue brush
Acrylic paint
Paintbrush
Compass
Star stickers
Paper fastener
Gemstones
Badge pin
Electrical tape

1 Ask an adult to cut a door in the front of the matchbox, using a craft knife and ruler. Leave one edge uncut. Cover the box with masking tape to make it stronger, including the cut edges.

2 Cover the box with shiny paper. Use white glue to stick down the edges and ends. Let dry.

3 Paint the inside of the box and let the paint dry.

4 Ask an adult to make a hole in the door with a compass. Push the paper fastener through to make a door knob. Stick the stars onto the front of the door.

5 Glue the gemstones around the door frame to decorate.

6 Glue the badge pin onto the back of the badge. Let it dry, and secure with electrical tape.

21

Little House

Make a friend or member of your family a model of their house. Remember to ask an adult to remove the matches from the matchbox before you start.

YOU WILL NEED
Matchbox
Masking tape
Pencil
Cardboard
Scissors
Colored felt
White glue and glue brush
Acrylic paints
Paintbrush
Colored paper
Fabric paint
Badge pin
Electrical tape

1 Stick masking tape around the matchbox to make it stronger. Draw a roof shape onto a piece of cardboard and cut it out.

2 Cut out a piece of colored felt to fit over the matchbox, and glue it on. While it is drying, paint both sides of the roof. Let dry before painting on a roof tile design in black paint.

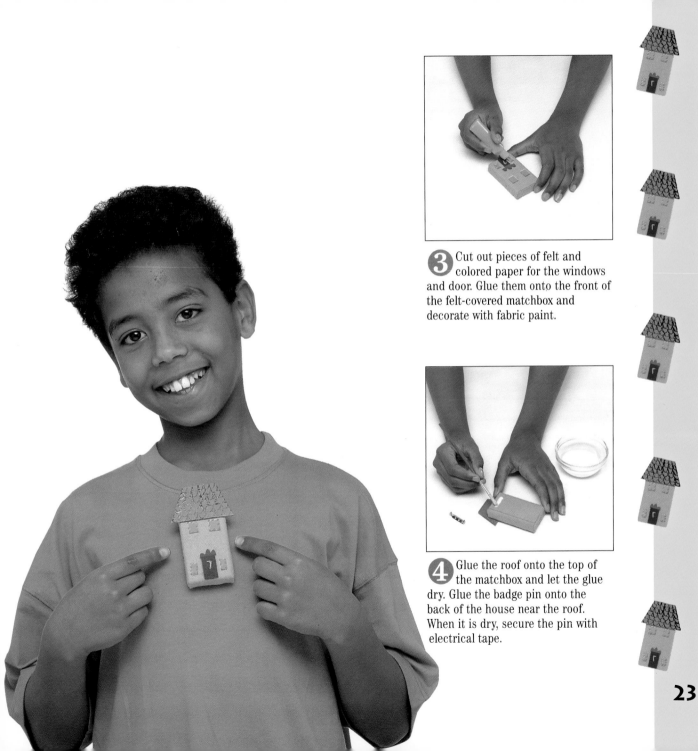

3 Cut out pieces of felt and colored paper for the windows and door. Glue them onto the front of the felt-covered matchbox and decorate with fabric paint.

4 Glue the roof onto the top of the matchbox and let the glue dry. Glue the badge pin onto the back of the house near the roof. When it is dry, secure the pin with electrical tape.

Birthday Parcel

This birthday badge makes an ideal present for a friend's birthday. It can be easily attached to a birthday card for a wonderful surprise.

YOU WILL NEED

Pencil
Coloured card
Ruler
Scissors
Coloured ribbons
PVA glue and glue brush
Coloured paper
Badge pin
Electrical tape

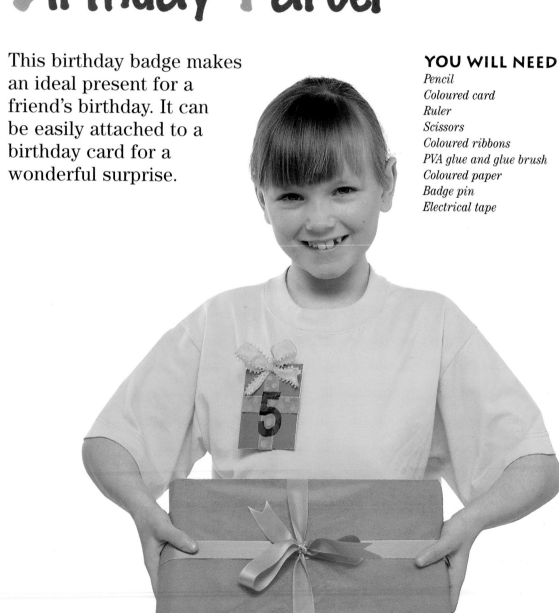

1 Cut out a piece of colored cardboard 3 inches by 3½ inches. Cut two lengths of ribbon that are just long enough to overlap the edges of the present. Glue them around the cardboard.

2 Draw and cut out your chosen number from a piece of colored paper (shiny paper is best), and glue it onto the present shape. Cut out small dots of colored paper and glue them onto the ribbon with little dabs of glue.

3 Tie a piece of brightly colored ribbon in a bow and glue it at the top of the present. Press down hard for a few minutes to allow the glue to set.

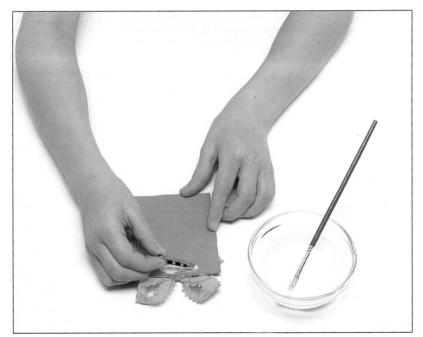

4 Cut a colored piece of paper to cover the back of the present and glue it on. Glue the badge pin on at the top of the present. When the glue has dried, secure the pin with electrical tape.

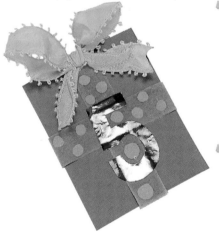

25

Driftwood Boat

This boat badge can be made from wood you have found on the beach or in the park, but make sure you sand the sides and surface well with sandpaper to avoid any splinters.

YOU WILL NEED

Small piece of wood
Sandpaper
Acrylic paint
Paintbrush
Thick cardboard
Ruler
Pencil
Scissors
Scrap of felt
Badge pin
Electrical tape

1 Find a small piece of wood and smooth the sides and surface with a piece of sandpaper. Paint a stripe along one side of the wood in acrylic paint and let it dry.

2 For the mast, cut a thick piece of cardboard ¼ inch wide and 2 inches long. Paint the cardboard a bright color. When the paint has dried, paint stripes in a different color across the cardboard.

3 Draw a sail shape on a piece of cardboard. Cut out the sail and glue it onto the mast. Cut out a small felt star and glue it onto one side of the sail.

4 Glue the mast onto the back of the wooden boat. Press down hard for a few minutes to let the glue set. Let the glue dry.

5 Glue the badge pin onto the back of the wooden boat. When the glue has dried, secure your pin with electrical tape.

Crown Frame

When you're not wearing this badge, you can hang it on your bedroom wall or door.

YOU WILL NEED

Pencil
Cardboard
Scissors
Newspaper
White glue and glue brush
Acrylic paint and paintbrush
Fake colored fur
Gemstones
Ruler
Badge pin
Electrical tape

1 Draw a crown shape on a piece of cardboard. Draw a circle in the center of the crown. Cut out the crown and the circle. Cover the crown with four layers of papier-mâché and leave to dry overnight.

2 Paint both sides of the crown gold and let the paint dry.

3 Cut a piece of fur the same size as the bottom of the crown and glue it on. Glue a gemstone onto each point of the crown.

4 Cut a piece of cardboard 2 inches by 2 inches. Paint a line of glue along *three* sides of the square, and glue it onto the back of the badge, covering the hole. Paint the cardboard gold. When the paint has dried, put a small photo or a picture from a magazine in the frame.

5 Attach the badge pin to the back of the badge using white glue and electrical tape.

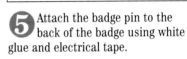

29

Felt Scotty Dog

Felt is a very easy material to cut, and the edges don't fray. Why not make this little dog and other felt friends, such as a cat or a rabbit?

YOU WILL NEED
Pencil
Tracing paper
Paper
Scissors
Pins
Felt
Needle
Thread
Badge pin
Ribbon

HANDY HINT
If you prefer, you can glue rather than sew the badge pin and bow to the felt. You could also glue the two felt pieces of the dog together, but remember to wait until the glue has thoroughly dried before you try on the badge.

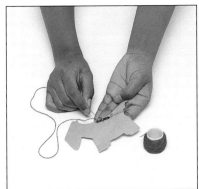

1 Trace the scotty dog template and transfer the shape onto a piece of paper. Cut out the shape and pin the paper to a piece of felt and cut around it carefully. Repeat using another piece of felt in a different color.

2 Sew the badge pin onto the back of one of the scotty dog pieces of felt using a needle and thread. You might want to ask an adult to help you do this.

3 Tie a piece of ribbon into a bow. Sew the bow onto the neck of the other scotty dog piece.

4 Pin the two scotty dog pieces together. Sew them together with a running stitch.

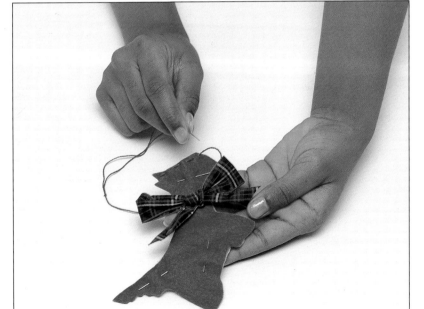

Clock Badge

You can control time yourself with this portable clock – just twist the arms around. It makes the perfect present for someone who likes to be on time!

YOU WILL NEED
Pencil
Compass
Ruler
Cardboard
Scissors
Acrylic paints
Paintbrush
Paper fastener
White glue and glue brush
Badge pin
Electrical tape

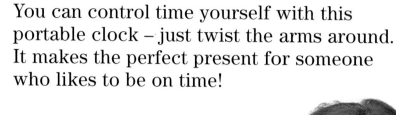

1 Draw a circle, approximately 6 inches across, with a compass on a piece of cardboard. Cut it out.

2 Paint the cardboard a bright color and paint a different colored outline around the edge of the circle. Let the paint dry.

3 Draw the numbers on the clock. Use a pencil first and then paint over them.

4 Draw two clock hands on a piece of cardboard. Cut out the hands and paint them. Ask an adult to make a hole at the bottom of each hand with a compass.

5 Ask an adult to make a hole in the center of the clock with a compass. Fasten the hands to the clock with the paper fastener.

6 Glue the badge pin onto the back of the clock behind the number 12. Let the glue dry before securing the pin with electrical tape.

Clay Fish

This clay fish is really colorful and is guaranteed to brighten up any outfit.

YOU WILL NEED

Pencil
Cardboard
Scissors
Ruler
Rolling pin
Self-hardening clay
Modeling tool
Acrylic paints
Paintbrush
White glue and
  glue brush
Badge pin
Electrical
  tape

HANDY HINT

If you are unable to buy the self-hardening clay, you can use another modeling material such as fimo or salt dough.

1 Draw a fish on cardboard and cut it out. Don't forget the fins and the tail. Roll out a piece of clay 4 inches by 4 inches. The clay should be approximately ¼ inch thick. Place the template on the clay and cut around it using a modeling tool.

2 Mark features and patterns on the fish with the sharp point of a modeling tool. When you have decorated the clay, leave it to harden in a dry place overnight.

3 Paint the fish with lots of bright colors. Don't forget to paint the back of the fish. Let each color dry before painting over it.

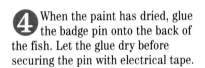

4 When the paint has dried, glue the badge pin onto the back of the fish. Let the glue dry before securing the pin with electrical tape.

35

Glitzy Star

This dazzling badge is decorated with candy wrappers. Wear the badge at parties and watch the sequins sparkle!

1 Draw a star on a piece of cardboard. Cut out the star and cover it with approximately three layers of papier-mâché. Allow the star to dry overnight in a warm place.

2 Smooth out the candy wrappers and glue them onto the front and back of the star.

3 Decorate the star by gluing on gemstones, sequins and glitter. Let the glue dry.

4 Glue a badge pin onto the back of the badge and let it dry before securing it with electrical tape.

Animals in a Field

This badge is full of surprises! Open the drawer of the box to reveal mini farm animals. You could also keep candy or other treasures in it for safekeeping.

YOU WILL NEED

Matchbox
Scissors
Grass paper
White glue and glue brush
Scraps of felt
Small plastic animals
Badge pin
Electrical tape

1 Cover both the outside of the matchbox and the inside drawer with grass paper, gluing it down smoothly.

2 Cut out tiny felt flowers, making the centers a different color from the petals. Glue the centers onto the flowers and let dry. Glue the flowers onto the outside of the matchbox.

3 Glue the plastic animals onto the top of the matchbox with white glue and hold them in place until they feel secure. Place the smaller animals in the drawer.

4 Glue the badge pin onto the back of the box. Let the glue dry before securing the pin with electrical tape.

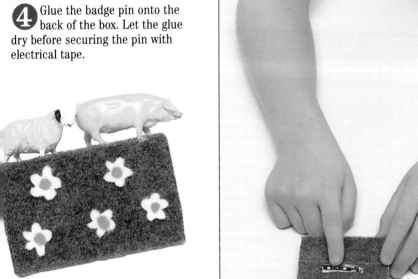

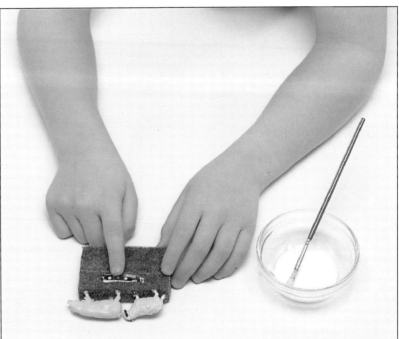

Fuzzy Orange

This brightly colored orange will lend a summery feel to your clothes. As well as an orange, you could make other fruity badges for your friends.

YOU WILL NEED

Pencil
Cardboard
Scissors
Acrylic paint
Paintbrush
White glue and glue brush
Orange yarn
Green felt
Fabric paint
Badge pin
Electrical tape

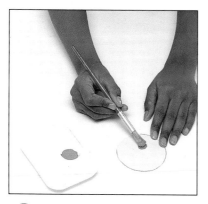

1 Draw a circle on a piece of cardboard and cut it out. Paint the circle orange and let it dry.

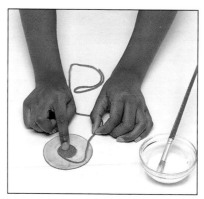

2 Cover the orange with white glue. Cut a long piece of orange yarn and, starting in the middle of the circle, carefully coil the yarn around itself until you have completely covered the cardboard.

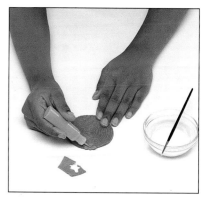

3 Cut out a small, starred leaf shape from green felt and glue it to the top of the orange. Dab on a blob of fabric paint where the stalk would be.

4 When the glue has dried, turn the badge over and glue the badge pin onto the back. Let the glue dry before securing the pin with electrical tape.

Salt Dough Badges

These badges are
nice and small, so
you can make a few
of them and wear
them together.
They are great
for brightening
up a hat, a bag
or a sweatshirt.

YOU WILL NEED

Rolling pin
Salt dough
Cookie cutters
Cookie sheet
Sandpaper
Acrylic paints
Paintbrush
White glue and glue brush
Small badge pins
Electrical tape

① Roll out the dough and cut out some shapes. Ask an adult to put them onto a greased cookie sheet and bake in the oven for about six hours at 250°F.

② When the shapes have baked, allow them to cool completely. Then gently rub the surfaces with sandpaper to make them smooth.

③ Paint the badges all over in a bright color. When the first coat of paint has dried, paint on some patterns.

④ Glue a small badge pin onto the back of each badge. Let the glue dry before securing the pin with electrical tape.

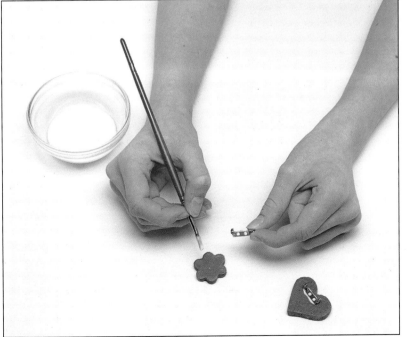

HANDY HINT

Save any leftover dough and store it in the fridge in a plastic bag to use later.

43

Bow Tie

Wear this snazzy bow tie to a costume party as part of a clown's outfit, or give it to a friend or member of your family as a fun clothes accessory.

YOU WILL NEED
Pencil
Cardboard
Scissors
Pins
Felt
Fabric glue and glue brush
Needle
Thread
Badge pin
Stuffing or scrunched-up
    tissue paper

44

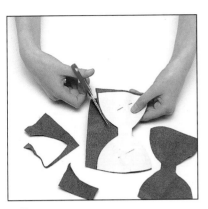

1 Draw a bow tie shape on a piece of cardboard and cut it out. Pin the shape onto a piece of felt, and cut around it carefully. Repeat with another piece of felt.

2 Cut out an assortment of colored felt dots, and glue them onto one of the felt bow tie pieces. Let the glue dry.

3 On the other piece of felt, sew on the badge pin in the center of the bow tie. Ask an adult to help if you find this difficult.

4 Sew the two pieces of felt together around the edge with a running stitch. Leave a small opening at one end through which to put the stuffing.

5 Fill the bow tie with the stuffing, using a pencil to help you push it carefully into the corners. Sew up the gap. You are now ready to dress up!

Flower Power Badge

The flowers in this badge are plastic, so they will last forever. This badge makes a great present for a friend.

YOU WILL NEED

Pencil
Cardboard
Scissors
Acrylic paint
Paintbrush
Plastic flowers
White glue and glue brush
Badge pin
Electrical tape

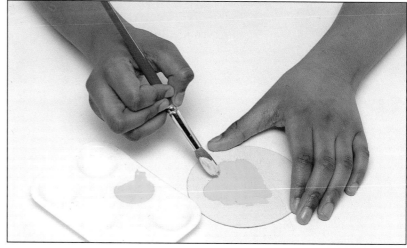

1 Draw a circle on a piece of cardboard, cut it out and paint it a bright color. Let the paint dry.

2 Glue a selection of plastic flowers onto the cardboard with white glue. Try to use a mixture of different flower shapes.

3 Cover the whole piece of cardboard with the flowers. Press the flowers down firmly until they feel secure. Let the glue dry.

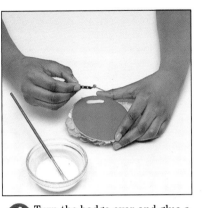

4 Turn the badge over and glue a colored circle of cardboard onto the back. Let it dry before gluing on the badge pin and securing the pin with electrical tape.

Fluffy Snowman

This snowman is wrapped up in a scarf to keep him warm. If you don't have any cotton, you could use scrunched-up white tissue paper instead.

YOU WILL NEED

Pencil
Cardboard
Scissors
White glue and glue brush
Cotton
Felt-tip pen
Felt
Badge pin
Electrical tape

1 Draw a snowman shape on a piece of cardboard. Cut it out.

2 Cover one side of the cardboard with white glue and press cotton onto the surface. Press hard and allow plenty of time for the glue to dry.

3 Draw features for the face and clothes of the snowman on felt using a felt-tip pen. Cut out the details and glue them in place on the cotton using white glue. To make a striped scarf, cut a length of felt and glue on some narrow strips of different-colored felt.

4 Glue colored cardboard onto the back of your snowman. Glue the badge pin behind the snowman's head. Let the glue dry before securing the pin with electrical tape.

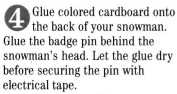

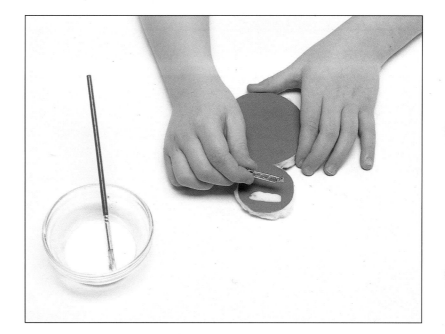

Happy Face

Brighten up your day by wearing this smiling badge. Hair made out of pipe cleaners gives it a really wacky look.

YOU WILL NEED

Pencil
Ruler
Compass
Cardboard
Scissors
Felt-tip pen
Felt
Double-sided tape
White glue and glue brush
Fabric paints
Colored pipe cleaners
Colored paper
Badge pin
Electrical tape

① Draw and cut out a circle approximately 5 inches wide on cardboard using a compass and pencil. With a felt-tip pen, draw another circle, ½ inch bigger than the cardboard circle, on felt and cut out the felt circle. Use double-sided tape to stick the cardboard circle in the middle of the felt circle. Make several cuts in the felt border surrounding the cardboard circle.

② Fold over the snipped pieces of felt onto the back of the cardboard and glue them down using white glue.

③ Cut out two ovals of felt for the eyes and glue them onto the face. Decorate the eyes with fabric paint. Paint on a nose and a mouth.

④ Coil some pipe cleaners around a pencil to make them curly, and stick them on the top of the head with white glue. Hold each pipe cleaner in place for a couple of minutes to allow the glue to set.

⑤ Cut a piece of colored paper the same size as the face, and glue it onto the back. Glue the badge pin onto the back of the cardboard behind the top of the face. Let the glue dry before securing the pin with electrical tape.

Lollipop Badge

This badge looks so tasty you almost want to eat it! However, although you have used real candy to make it, you must not eat it because it has been covered with varnish.

1 Draw a circle on cardboard, using a compass, and cut it out. The circle should be about 8 inches in diameter.

2 Paint the circle a bright color on both sides. Let dry.

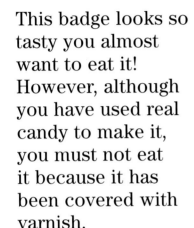

YOU WILL NEED
Pencil
Compass
Cardboard
Ruler
Scissors
Acrylic paint
Paintbrush
White glue and glue brush
Hard candy
Varnish and brush
Felt
Ribbon
Badge pin
Electrical tape

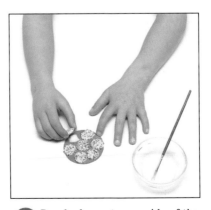

3 Brush glue onto one side of the cardboard circle and glue on the candy. When the glue has dried, paint over the candy with varnish.

4 When the varnish is completely dry, cut a strip of felt 1½ inches by ½ inch. Glue it behind the badge. This is the stick.

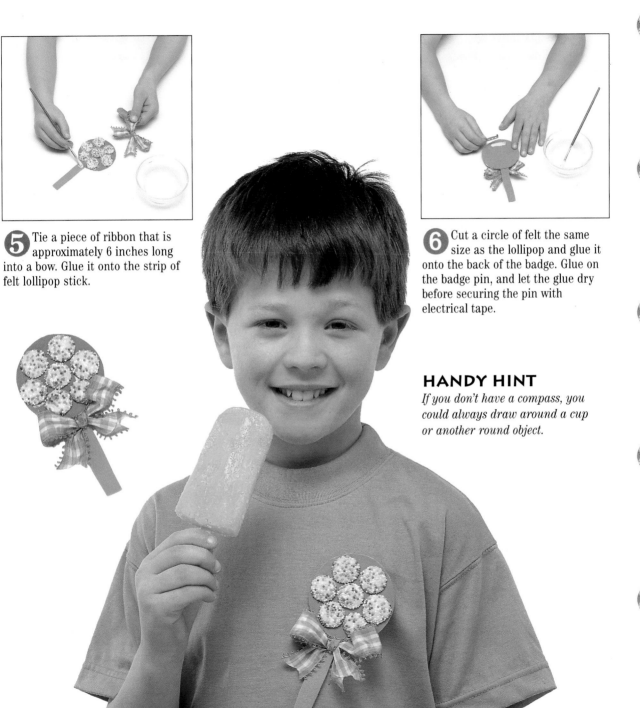

5 Tie a piece of ribbon that is approximately 6 inches long into a bow. Glue it onto the strip of felt lollipop stick.

6 Cut a circle of felt the same size as the lollipop and glue it onto the back of the badge. Glue on the badge pin, and let the glue dry before securing the pin with electrical tape.

HANDY HINT
If you don't have a compass, you could always draw around a cup or another round object.

53

Butterfly

This beautiful salt dough butterfly will really liven up a hat or a shirt, and is perfect for any spring outfit. Salt dough is also very cheap and easy to make.

YOU WILL NEED

Pencil
Cardboard
Scissors
Rolling pin
Salt dough
Ruler
Modeling tool
Water
Baking tray
Sandpaper
Acrylic paint
Paintbrush
Gem stones
White glue
  and glue brush
Badge pin
Electrical tape

1 Draw a butterfly shape on a piece of cardboard. Cut it out. Roll out a piece of salt dough on a flour-dusted surface to approximately ½ inch thick. Place the butterfly on the dough and cut around it using a modeling tool.

2 Make features on your butterfly with the modeling tool. Stick on dough pieces, using water as a dough glue.

3 Ask an adult to bake it for about six hours at 250°F. When the butterfly has cooled, sand down any rough edges.

4 Paint patterns on the butterfly. When the paint has dried, glue a gemstone onto either side of the wing. Glue a badge pin on the back. When the glue has dried, secure the pin with electrical tape.

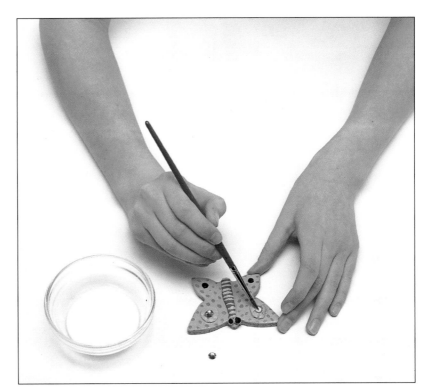

HANDY HINT

If you don't have any modeling tools, you could always use the tip of a pencil or the edge of a ruler to shape and cut the salt dough.

Paper Flower

This paper flower is a great way to jazz up any outfit, but be careful, as it will tear easily. You could make more flowers in different colors and join them to make a bunch.

YOU WILL NEED

Pencil
Thin cardboard
Tracing paper
Scissors
Colored crêpe paper
Compass
Pipe cleaner
Felt
Ruler
White glue and glue brush
Fabric paint
Needle
Thread
Badge pin

1 Draw a flower template on thin cardboard and transfer it onto three pieces of different colored crêpe paper.

2 Ask an adult to use the compass to make a hole in the center of each flower shape, then thread the pipe cleaner through each one. Coil up the ends of the pipe cleaners to make the centers of the flowers.

3 Scrunch the flower together a little to make it look natural. Cut a strip of felt approximately 8 inches long and 1 inch wide. Brush glue onto one side of the strip of felt and stick one end onto the back of the flower. Wrap the rest of the felt strip tightly around the pipe cleaner and secure. Let dry.

4 Draw and cut out two identical leaf shapes from felt. Glue a leaf onto either side of the stem of the flower. Paint in the veins of the leaf with fabric paint.

5 Sew the badge pin onto the top of the felt flower stem. If you find this difficult, ask an adult to help.

Birthday Badge

What could be a better present for one of your friends than a personalized birthday badge?

YOU WILL NEED
Pencil
Paper
Scissors
Rolling pin
Fimo
Ruler
Modeling tool
Cookie cutter
Cookie sheet
White glue and glue brush
Badge pin
Electrical tape

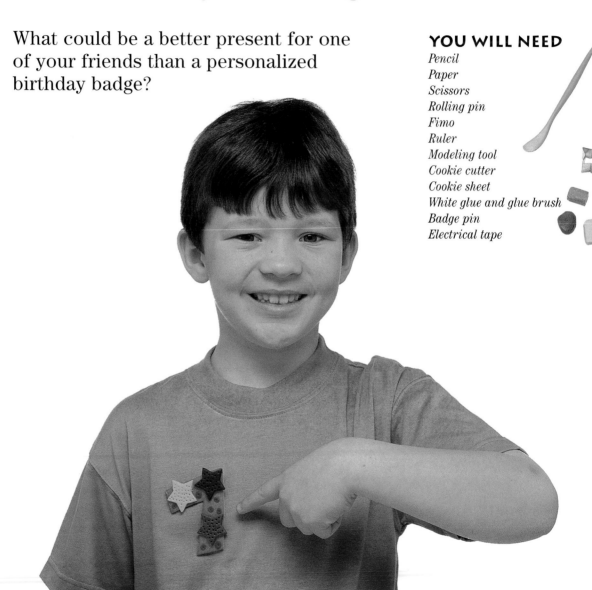

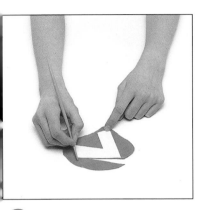

1 Draw your chosen number on a piece of paper and cut it out. Use a rolling pin to roll out a piece of fimo to approximately ¼ inch thick. Place your template on it and cut around it using a modeling tool.

2 Roll out a piece of fimo in a contrasting color to the number, and cut out shapes, such as a star, using a cookie cutter. Stick the stars on the number with glue.

3 Decorate the rest of the number with the modeling tool. Carefully put the fimo shape onto a cookie sheet. Ask an adult to bake the fimo in the oven. Read the instructions on the fimo package to check how long it should bake.

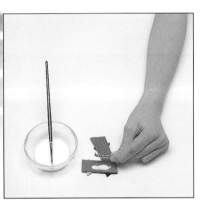

4 When the fimo has completely cooled, glue the badge pin onto the back of your badge. Let it dry completely before securing with electrical tape.

Button Heart

This badge makes a terrific present for someone special on Valentine's Day.

YOU WILL NEED
Pencil
Cardboard
Scissors
Acrylic paint
Paintbrush
Buttons
White glue and glue brush
Ribbon
Ruler
Colored tape
Needle
Thread
Badge pin

1 Draw a heart shape on a piece of cardboard. Cut it out and paint it on both sides.

2 When the paint has dried, glue the buttons onto one side of the heart using white glue.

3 Tie a piece of ribbon approximately 10 inches in length in a bow. Glue the two ends of the ribbon onto the back of the heart. Let the glue dry. Stick a piece of colored tape over the ribbon.

4 Sew the badge pin onto the back of the ribbon bow. Ask an adult to help if you find this too hard.

HANDY HINT

When buying the white cardboard, ask for some that is thin enough to cut with scissors, yet stiff enough to stand up straight.

61

Dotty Dinosaur

Make this dotty dinosaur out of fimo.
If you don't have any fimo, use
another modeling material
such as salt dough or
self-hardening clay.

YOU WILL NEED

Pencil
Cardboard
Scissors
Rolling pin
Fimo
Ruler
Modeling tool
White glue and glue brush
Cookie sheet
Badge pin
Electrical tape

62

1 Draw a dinosaur shape on cardboard and cut it out. Using a rolling pin, roll out a piece of fimo to approximately ¼ inch thick. Place the template on the fimo and cut around it using a modeling tool.

2 Cut out some feet and glue them to the dinosaur. Now cut out spikes in a contrasting color fimo and glue them onto the dinosaur's body.

3 Roll out tiny spots of fimo and glue them onto the body. Ask an adult to bake the fimo in the oven. Read the instructions on the packet to check how long it should bake for.

4 When the fimo has completely cooled, glue the badge pin onto the back using white glue. Let the glue dry before securing the pin with electrical tape.

ACKNOWLEDGMENTS

The publishers would like to thank the following children for modeling for this book, and their parents and Walnut Tree Walk Primary School for making it possible for them to do so:

Danny Bill
Emma Currie
Vicky Dummigan
Kirsty Fraser
Cherine Henry
Barry Lee
Kirsty Lee
Mickey Malku
Sharday Manahan
Nancy Miller
Letitia Williams